Helping Children
With Feelings

Helping Chila...
who Bottle Up
their Feelings

A Nifflenoo Called
Nevermind

A Guidebook

Helping Children who Bottle Up their Feelings

A Nifflenoo Called Nevermind

A Guidebook

Margot Sunderland

Illustrated by

Nicky Armstrong

Routledge
Taylor & Francis Group

LONDON AND NEW YORK

Note on the Text
For the sake of clarity alone, throughout the text the child has been referred to as 'he' and the parent as 'she'.

Unless otherwise stated, for clarity alone, where 'mummy', 'mother' or 'mother figure' is used, this refers to either parent or other primary caretaker.

Confidentiality
Where appropriate, full permission has been granted by adults, or children and their parents, to use clinical material. Other illustrations comprise synthesised and disguised examples to ensure anonymity.

First published by 2000 by Speechmark Publishing Ltd

Published 2017 by Routledge
2 Park Square, Milton Park, Abingdon, Oxon OX14 4RN
711 Third Avenue, New York, NY 10017, USA

Routledge is an imprint of the Taylor & Francis Group, an informa business

British Library Cataloguing in Publication Data
Sunderland, Margot
  A Nifflenoo Called Nevermind : helping children who bottle up their
  feelings Guidebook. – (Stories for troubled children)
  1. Storytelling – Therapeutic use 2. Child psychology 3. Learning,
  Psychology of
  I. Title II. Armstrong, Nicky
  615.8'516

ISBN-13: 978-8-6388457-3 (pbk)

Contents

ABOUT THE AUTHOR

MARGOT SUNDERLAND is Founding Director of the Centre for Child Mental Health, London. She is also Head of the Children and Young People Section of The United Kingdom Association for Therapeutic Counselling. In addition, she formed the research project, 'Helping Where it Hurts' which offers free therapy and counselling to troubled children in several primary schools in North London. She is a registered Integrative Arts Psychotherapist and registered Child Therapeutic Counsellor, Supervisor and Trainer.

Margot is also Principal of The Institute for Arts in Therapy and Education – a fully accredited Higher Education College running a Diploma course in Child Therapy and Masters Degree courses in Arts Psychotherapy and Arts in Education and Therapy.

Margot is a published poet and author of two non-fiction books – one on *Dance* (Routledge Theatre Arts, New York and J Garnet Miller, England) and the other called *Draw on Your Emotions* (Speechmark Publishing/Winslow Press, Bicester and Erickson, Italy).

ABOUT THE ILLUSTRATOR

NICKY ARMSTRONG holds an MA from The Slade School of Fine Art and a BA Hons in Theatre Design from the University of Central England. She is currently teacher of trompe l'œil at The Hampstead School of Decorative Arts, London. She has achieved major commissions nationally and internationally in mural work and fine art.

ACKNOWLEDGEMENTS

A special acknowledgement to Mattan Lederman who, at age seven, drew an entire set of pictures for all of the five stories in the pack. Several of his ideas and designs were then adopted by the illustrator.

I would like to thank Katherine Pierpont, Charlotte Emmett and Ruth Bonner for all their superb skill and rigour in the editing process, and for making the long writing journey such a pleasurable one.

I would also like to thank all the children, trainees and supervisees with whom I have worked, whose poetry, images and courage have greatly enriched both my work and my life.

ABOUT THIS GUIDEBOOK

If a child is going to benefit from the full therapeutic potential of *A Nifflenoo Called Nevermind*, this accompanying guidebook will be a vital resource. We strongly advise that you read it before reading the story itself to the child. By doing so, you will come to the child from a far more informed position, and so you will be able to offer him a far richer, and more empathic, response.

This guidebook details the common psychological origins and most relevant psychotherapeutic theories for the problems and issues addressed in the story. If you read it before reading the story to the child, it will prevent your coming to the child from an ignorant or closed viewpoint about why he is troubled. For example, 'I'm sure that Johnny's school work, has gone downhill because he is missing his Daddy, who moved out a few months ago' may be an accurate or inaccurate hypothesis. There may be many other reasons for Johnny's problems with his school work which have not been considered. The problem may well be complex, as are so many psychological problems. Coming from a closed or too narrow viewpoint all too often means that the helping adult is in danger of projecting on to the child *their own* feelings and views about the world.

Very few parents are consciously cruel. When something goes wrong in the parenting of a child, it is often to do with the parent *not knowing* about some vital aspect of child psychology or child development, or a lack in the way the parent was brought up themselves. There is still a tragic gap between what is known about effective parenting in child psychology, psychotherapy and scientific research, and how much of this is communicated to parents via parenting books, or through television and the press. So this guidebook is not about blaming parents. Rather, the aim is to support. More generally, the aim is to heighten the awareness of *anyone* looking after children about how things can go wrong (usually despite the best intentions), and about how to help them go right in the first place, or to get mended if they do go wrong.

This guide book includes what children themselves have said about what it is like trying to cope with the problems and issues addressed in the story, and describes the stories they have enacted through their play. It also includes a section which offers suggestions and ideas for things to say and things to do after you have read *A Nifflenoo Called Nevermind* to the child. The suggestions and ideas are specifically designed to help a child to think about, express and further digest his feelings about the problems and issues addressed in the story. Some of the exercises are also designed to inspire children to speak more about what they are feeling through *their own* spontaneous story-making.

Everyday language is not the natural language for children to use to speak about what they feel. But, with an adult they trust, they can usually show or enact, draw or play out their feelings very well indeed. Therefore, many of the exercises offered in this guidebook will support the child in creative, imaginative and playful ways of expressing himself. Also, so that you avoid asking too many questions, interrogating the child about his feeling life (to which children do not respond at all well) some of the exercises simply require from the child to tick a box, 'show me', or pick a word or an image from a selection.

INTRODUCTION

What the story is about

Nevermind the Nifflenoo always soldiers on, regardless. Each time something horrible happens to him, he is very brave and says, 'Never mind!' He meets with all sorts of setbacks, disappointments and bullying, but each time he just puts his feelings away, puts on a brave face and gets on with his life.

The trouble is that, after a while, he is so full of bottled-up feelings that he gets stuck in a hedge. What is more, some of his feelings start to leak out of him in ways that hurt the people around him. Luckily, however, along comes a bogwert who helps Nevermind to see that his feelings really *do* matter, and should not be ignored or pushed down. Nevermind then learns how to express his feelings and to tell someone about them, rather than trying to deal with them all by himself. He also learns how to stand up for himself and say, 'I *do* mind!'

The main psychological messages in this story

Bottling up uncomfortable feelings does not mean that they go away. In fact, they tend to get bigger and stronger inside because of all the pressure of being bottled up.

Bottled-up feelings leak out through neurotic symptoms, physical illness or acting-out behaviour, causing suffering to oneself and often to others. It is exactly like the rule in science that energy can never be killed off, only diverted.

Bottled-up feelings can eclipse pleasure and enjoyment in life.

A world of unshared emotionality can be very lonely and frightening because, in their unshared state, painful feelings tend to grow in size.

If you tell someone about your painful feelings, it can take the hugeness, the scariness and the pain out of them, and make them far more manageable.

You can ask for help with your bottled-up feelings from someone who can understand. You do not have to 'soldier on' with them alone.

Paying little or no attention, or distracting yourself from your difficult feelings, does not make them go away. Why carry around with you the baggage of your past, when with some help you can put it down, and truly live in your present?

Who the story is for

This story was written for all the following:

Children who are trying to manage their too painful feelings by themselves.

Children who do not let themselves cry, protest or say that they are scared.

Children living with too many unresolved painful emotions from the past.

Children whose lives are full of disturbing, overwhelming or confusing experiences, which they have been unable to think through or feel through properly.

Children who are full of unexpressed feelings because expressing them feels far too dangerous. (As one little boy said, 'If I was to get angry in here, I think it would make all the windows break and the ceiling fall down.')

Children who are trying to manage far more than they can actually manage.

Children who are full of unmourned grief.

> You think I'll weep.
> No, I'll not weep.
> *[Storm within]*
> I have full cause of weeping, but this heart
> Shall break into a hundred thousand flaws
> Or ere I'll weep – O fool, I shall go mad!
> (Shakespeare, *King Lear*, I(7), 441-45)

WHAT LIFE IS LIKE FOR CHILDREN WHO HAVE DECIDED TO KEEP THEIR TROUBLED FEELINGS AS A PRIVATE AFFAIR

> **George, aged 4**
>
> I don't need my Mummy very much.

Winnicott, the psychoanalyst, coined the phrase 'self-holding'. Self-holding means dealing with painful or difficult feelings all on your own, as opposed to asking for help with them. So self-holding children are those who have stopped, or never started, reaching out when they are distressed. As a result, they have adopted an attitude equivalent to an adult's 'Stiff upper lip', 'Grin and bear it', 'Best foot forward'.

So, although self-holding children may appear outwardly sociable and friendly, their feeling self is very much a private affair. By and large, it does not occur to children who self-hold to tell someone that they are unhappy, frightened, enraged and so on. In fact, many of them are convinced that asking for help with their feelings is a very bad idea, and would just make them feel worse rather than better; that, by telling, they would end up feeling ashamed, embarrassed, rejected or misunderstood. This basic mistrust can continue throughout their lives. Furthermore, a world which is seen as having no helpers that actually 'help' is a very bleak and desolate world to be in. Indeed, in their play in therapy, many self-holding children show help rendered impotent. (See Figure 1, a sandplay story in which the emergency services and the school crossing patrol lady are rendered impotent and so never reach the people who need help.)

Other children (for example, children with depressed or emotionally volatile parents) think that telling their feelings would somehow damage the person they tell. Such children believe that their feelings are 'bigger' than the capacity of the adults in their lives to contain them. So they make a decision early on (usually out of their conscious awareness) to manage their feelings all by themselves.

Self-holding children often give out the message, 'I don't need you' or, even simpler, 'I don't need'. This can become so ingrained in their way of being in the world that they themselves can come to believe it too.

Adults who established patterns of self-holding in childhood said the following:

'It never occurred to me to tell my mother that for all my childhood I was terrified of the dark.'

'It never occurred to me to tell Daddy that I was terrified of Mummy.'

'I never thought to say to my parents that I was deeply unhappy at school.'

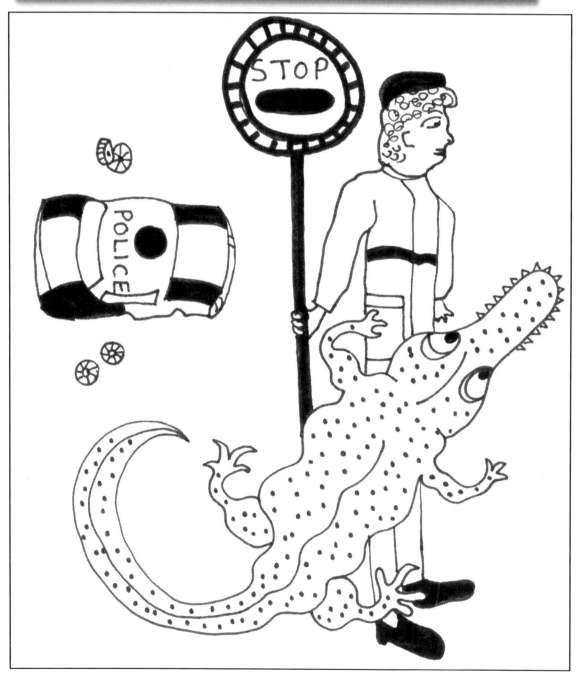

Figure 1 When helpers don't help

What life is like for children who are bottling up far too many difficult feelings

In the first place, bottling up feelings is stressful and very hard work. The inner pressure from trying to keep them bottled up as opposed to expressing them, can feel awful. The need to discharge the tension in some way becomes more and more urgent as the mind is naturally pushing to unburden itself.

Quite simply, bottling up feelings is a lousy way of trying to manage them. This is because bottled-up feelings are not dormant. As Freud said, they just 'proliferate in the dark' (Freud, 1915). So self-holding in children is always a drastic failure. Such children will sooner or later show signs of 'emotional leaking'. The tension from the ever-increasing pressure inside starts to leak out. Children simply do not have the internal resources to manage their troubled feelings on their own.

Second, when bottled-up feelings leak out, they do so in all manner of ways:

Agitation, anxiety, worry

Having an 'accident'

Acting-out/conduct disorders

Angry outbursts at the slightest thing or at entirely the wrong person, such as suddenly punching someone in the playground

Not being able to concentrate

Body problems – imagined or actual (preoccupation with 'something worrying inside me' or actual physical symptoms)

Bed-wetting

Soiling

Nightmares

Being sick

Social withdrawal

Phobias

Obsessions

Being 'all over the place' – spilling, dropping, forgetting or losing things

Hyperactivity, maniacally moving from one thing to another as a way of trying to run away from the ever-increasing internal pressure of too strong feeling. Some of these children are labelled as having ADHD (Attention Deficit Hyperactive Disorder). If they stayed still a while, or concentrated on just one thing, they might feel the too intense arousal of their painful feelings and be overwhelmed, or flooded by them.

It can be exhausting for people to be with children who are bottling up too many feelings. They can end up feeling the intense levels of anxiety from which the child is so desperate to get away. There are some children like Nevermind, who try to keep their leaking unnoticed. 'Well done!' some people might say, well done for keeping the lid so tightly on those feelings, without disturbing or hurting anyone. But the price these children can pay for no apparent leakage is often far too high. As one adolescent said, 'The way I dealt with the mess of my feelings was to keep quiet, but being quiet was just another mess.'

Although some 'self-holding' children may show no outward signs of leakage, inside they may be suffering from a great deal of private worry and anguish, catastrophising or depression. They are just better than most at disguising it.

> One question has led to so many other unresolved questions that he has willy-nilly gathered around himself some kind of fatal bog, some sort of stinking filth comprising his doubts, his emotions. (Dostoevsky, 1991, p14)

Third, some children try to deal with the pressure of too many bottled-up feelings in a variety of ways:

Swallowing down their feelings with food
Drinking them down
Eating them down and then vomiting them out (bulimia)
Television-watching them away
Blasting them away by playing very loud music
Sniffing them down (glue-sniffing)
Self-mutilating, to try to release some of the tension
Trying to think themselves out of their feelings, by living in their heads.

A fourth problem is that, when you are busy applying the emotional brakes, you are not really free to get on with anything else. As John, aged ten, said, 'There's like a traffic-jam of anger inside me, all furious, all piled up.' As it takes a great deal of energy to bottle up a too strong feeling, the child's attention to other things is often badly affected. Metaphorically speaking, when children sit on their feelings, they are not free to stand up and walk or dance into a different space. Bottled-up feelings cast a dark shadow over life. In this sense they are a very burdensome baggage. Bottled-up feelings hold a child in his past (recent or distant), so he is never free to be fully in his present. Going around with emotional brakes on all the time limits your capacity to play, to learn, to develop as a person. And it certainly saps life of a lot of its richness.

Fifth, it can be very lonely trying to manage all your feelings all by yourself. As Segal says, 'Many people never allow themselves to be put in a position where others might see "the mess inside" them . . . As a result, they never receive the reassurance of being "known" or "understood", and still loved, mess and all' (1985, p225). Holding on to all your troubled feelings is, in many ways, 'doing life on your own'. And when you never tell anyone how you feel, it often means never feeling that delicious sense of being comforted and warmed by another's genuine compassion and concern. A life devoid of comfort and concern can be acutely bleak and miserable.

The tragedy for children who self-hold is that they often have no living knowledge of what it is like to feel deeply understood by someone – and so it is not something they seek out. Furthermore, because they have never really shown their feeling self to anyone, many never feel really loved – because someone who says they love them does not really know them.

Furthermore, bottling up feelings can make it extremely difficult to concentrate on school work. Some children are suffering from so much emotional indigestion that they cannot possibly settle down to their work, just as it is extremely difficult to concentrate on anything properly if you have awful physical indigestion. Another analogy for trying to get on with life with emotional indigestion is that it is like trying to listen to a radio with noisy interference, but here the interference is painful mind noise. In fact, bottled-up feelings can take up so much space in a child's mind that there is little or no room left for any interested or enjoyed focus on anything else: 'A person who holds on "by the skin of his teeth" is desperate' (Lowen, 1975, p91).

So some children are far too full of feelings to be able to learn. They have no psychological space left in their minds for learning. Nothing can hope to compete with the sheer pull of the unexpressed feeling in the child's inner world when it is just too strong, too intense.

Imagine a child full of too much unexpressed anger or grief, standing in front of a magnificent sunset. He can look at it, but because his attention is on his emotional pain he does not really see it. His bottled-up feelings are too distracting a background. When emotional pain in a child's inner world is particularly strong, it can totally eclipse anything lovely in his world and deafen or blind him to it.

Tommy, aged five

Tommy was very depressed. His Daddy, whom he loved deeply, had moved out and was now living abroad. Tommy's mother said, 'All Tommy needs is to have a holiday by the seaside'. So she took Tommy to the beautiful seaside. It did not make the slightest impression on him. In his head he was with the images of Daddy shutting the door for the last time and Daddy getting on the aeroplane. While on the beach, he was not seeing the sea or the sand or the sun, he was seeing the images of Daddy in his head. The images in his inner world were stronger than those of the seaside. In fact, the painful Daddy images drowned the seaside out.

Tommy's mother had not understood the power of the inner world, how the inner world gives colour and meaning to events in the outer world, particularly if the inner world is flooded by unworked-through, too intense, too painful feelings.

> In Zen Buddhism . . . they say that the mind should be like an empty rice bowl. If it's already full, then the universe can't fill it. If it's empty, it has room to receive. (Williamson, 1990, p52)

Finally, 'self-holding' children can develop physical symptoms (real or imagined). A child can have conscious or unconscious fears of 'making a mess' emotionally, that is, a fear that all their bottled-up feelings will burst out. These fears can be displaced on to their body: so some children fear wetting or soiling themselves in public, fainting or being sick. In other words, fear of the body losing control in one of these ways is a transferred focus of fear for the real fear of losing control emotionally. The real fear has simply been wrongly labelled as something physical, which feels far less threatening. Fear of infection or contamination can be far more manageable than thinking that there is something out of control in your mind, that may suddenly burst out in uncontrollable rage or grief.

It is also now well established (see Martin, 1997, for an excellent collation of some of the most recent research on this) that bottling-up feelings can have a very bad effect on the immune system, causing actual illness. Furthermore, something in the body can actually start to 'break out', 'break down' or 'explode' from having been held in and held on to for so long. People who seep anger are at particular risk. A study by Williams (1989) shows that being prone to anger was a stronger predictor of dying young than were other risk factors such as smoking, high blood pressure and high cholesterol (Goleman, 1996, p170).

One five-year-old boy would vomit water three or four times a day at school. As soon as he started counselling, he stopped being sick. His stories were all about floods and avalanches. Because his counsellor could understand how desperate he was, and too full of painful feeling, he no longer needed to express this physically.

How aware are children that they are bottling up their feelings?

> A plague of sighing and grief – it blows a man up like a bladder. (Shakespeare, *Henry IV Part I*, II (5), 333).

If a child's defences are not working well, or if he has dared to stay open to his feelings, he may be painfully aware of carrying too many bottled-up feelings inside. A common 'play' theme in the therapy of such children is the theme of someone or something bursting or flooding because they are too full. In sandplay therapy, such children will often need to flood the sand tray. This is not being naughty, it is an essential communication about their inner world.

Here are some examples of stories told by children who were aware that they were struggling with too many bottled-up feelings:

Nettie, aged four

Nettie said to her teacher: 'I've got too many busy spiders in my tummy. They make me feel bad. When I cry they go away.'

Mary, aged eight

'The sky is full of poo. The little bird gets all muddled up in it and some of it gets right inside her . . . It is all very frightening.'

As this therapy unfolded it was clear that Mary (whose father had died), was talking about too many very sad feelings inside her that had built up and up. Because she had never had any help with these feelings, she now experienced them as toxic and dangerous.

Sally, aged twelve

Sally was referred for counselling because she was full of anxiety that was interfering with her schoolwork. Sally made a sandplay picture of a recurrent dream she had (see Figure 2). It was about rows and rows of toilets. All were full of poo, with handles that did not work. And so, each toilet she went to, she could not use because it was already full. Sally said she felt like that sometimes in real life: 'Just far too full of yuk.' Before counselling, she had absolutely no sense of anyone being able to help her 'contain' her feelings. Her mother was 'full' of her own deep depression and anxiety.

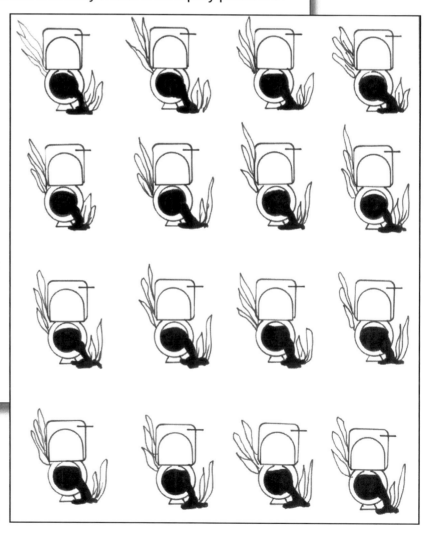

Figure 2

Sally's dream of rows and rows of too full toilets – an image of how no one was helping her to express and process her feelings

What children like 'Nevermind' fear will happen if they do express their feelings

I knew if I opened my mouth something terrible would dribble out . . . gush down the front of my shirt, over shoes and cover the carpet. (Galloway, 1996, p137)

Some children have a sense that feelings kept inside them for too long can go bad or rotten. This can be true, as in the case of anger, which when stored up for too long can turn to hate or bitterness. Similarly, resentment towards someone, when bottled up too long, can start to eat away at you and at the store of loving feelings you have.

It is very common for children who bottle up their feelings to fear disaster about what could happen if they were to express their feelings. This fear is what they use to justify to themselves that the best thing to do with feelings is to bottle them up. Common fears include the following:

Not being able to stop crying, if they let themselves start

Feeling overwhelmed in a too frightening, painful or out-of-control way

Hurting in some way the people they love the most

Exploding

Snapping

Spilling

Going mad

Lashing out

Causing a fire (metaphorically speaking or literally).

Figure 3 Bottled-up feelings eating away at you

In the story, Nevermind fears that, if he lets go of all his bottled-up feelings, there will be one almighty mess of flood and fire (Figure 4). Many children who have a fear of feeling flooded by too strong feeling in one of the ways detailed above, have *actually* felt flooded in this way in early infancy. The experience may well have been repressed (and so forgotten) because it was unbearable. Nevertheless, from the dark basement of their unconscious, it continues to haunt.

Nevermind said he could not possibly do that. 'I've so many uncried tears inside me,' he told the bogwert, 'that it would cause huge floods. I've so much anger that it would cause huge fires.'

Figure 4 Nevermind fears drowning in the flood of his own feeling

> At lunch time I went to the little park on 53rd Street and sat in a chair facing the waterfall that drowns the city noises, staring at the water falling endlessly down the smooth rock wall: all my tears. I cried, just a little, but inside I felt the endless waterfall, water falling . . . Waterfall, water wall. Water walling; water welling. Welling and falling. (Nakhla & Jackson, 1993, p49)

Such children feel too threatened by the idea of expressing their feelings as, on some level, they know they do not have the means to deal with their intense emotional arousal. By and large, such children have had all too little experience of feeling psychologically held by an understanding adult, and so of moving through an intense release of their feelings into a delicious sense of calm and relief. Sadly, the fear of some disastrous spilling or flooding, or fears of going mad, can lead to more and more desperate attempts to hold on or hold in, which simply makes the pressure worse.

Crying in the restaurant

I'm sorry for crying in your restaurant
But the river inside me's just burst its banks.
I know it isn't really done.
And the man with the Chicken Kiev
Looks extremely uncomfortable.
I can see that tears don't mix well with the Musak
But the level keeps rising in this merciless flood.

Apologies for saturating your serviettes
And having to pinch some from the next table.
I didn't realise before embarking on my avocado
The force of this deluge of rushing grief.

I do understand your clientele are here for the food,
And I'm serving them with a reminder
Of their own well deep weeping,
Which they're all somehow managing to control,
Far better than I.

Margot Sunderland

For other children, it is a somewhat different hopelessness, namely that of thinking, 'Even if I were to cry or get angry or say what I feel, I could never convey the depth of the pain I feel – so I may as well not speak at all.'

> Oh I have suffered
> More agony than all these tears can show.
> (Medea in *Euripedes*, 1994, p8)

Understanding why children bottle up their feelings, rather than telling someone about them

How a child's feelings can be driven underground by an inadequate parental response

> For human beings, not to speak is to die. (Pablo Neruda, 1975, p205)

If a parent is emotionally aware, and can consistently and reliably imagine herself into her child's mental state, that child is likely to want to talk about his painful or difficult feelings. He will want to talk about things which he finds frightening or disturbing. He will want to go over them again and again until they have been fully worked through. He will start to do this as soon as he can talk. The following are some examples of toddlers asking for help with their troubled feelings:

Lisa, aged eighteen months

Over a three-hour period after playgroup, Lisa kept saying, 'Ed-bus-ballo', 'Ed-bus-ballo'. She was so persistent and distressed that eventually her Daddy rang the play-leader to see if anything had happened during the day. The play-leader said there hadn't been anything, 'Oh, but she did seem upset when Edward burst her balloon.' When Daddy then told Lisa how sorry he was about her balloon and how sad it must have been to lose it like that, and how she may be feeling very angry with Edward for doing such a thing, the little girl started playing happily again. She had been given the 'help' she needed in the form of a real empathic understanding.

Sunita, aged three

Sunita had a fall and cut his leg quite badly. For the rest of the day he said repeatedly, 'Tell me again what happened today, Mummy – tell me again'. Luckily, Sunita had a mother who was prepared to go over the incident many times, empathising with his feelings of shock and fear and pain.

Amy, aged three

Amy was attacked by a bullying five-year-old in the playground. For the rest of the day she interrupted most activities and conversations with the remark, 'He was a big bad bully, wasn't he?' During her bedtime story, she was unable to concentrate and kept turning to her Mummy to say, 'He was a big bad bully, wasn't he?' When the little girl had taken in enough empathy from a variety of trusted adults in her life she got on with playing happily and no longer referred to the incident. The trauma had been properly processed. Thanks to the understanding adults in her life, her feelings about the experience did not need to be banished to her unconscious. The adults in her life had not told her to 'stop going on about it'. Rather, they listened and sympathised, and helped her go over and over the event.

The problem comes if a parent is not emotionally open to her child's feelings. The parent may be good in lots of areas of parenting – playing, physical care, fun, providing interesting activities, boundaries – but not good at helping the child with his feelings. She may, for example, not really notice a change in her child's mood state; not really register his sadness or feelings of hurt, say from feeling ousted by a sibling. Or she may repeatedly respond to her child's more vulnerable feelings with impatience or indifference. The child then gets the message that expressing softer, more tender feelings is shaming. Or she may tell the child who is disappointed or angry to cheer up, giving the message that it is not OK to have difficult or painful feelings. It is only OK to have nice, mild or happy ones.

A parent may also fail to notice that her child is expressing his love for her and so treads all over it. Here is an example:

> **Sascha, aged seven**
>
> Sascha remembered as a toddler bringing home a painting for his mother. It was a love gift. His mother said it was wet and would mess up her kitchen, so could he please take it out. He walked away with intense hurt and disappointment. His mother failed him twice. First she failed to respond to his love, and second she failed to notice his hurt as he walked away from her, crestfallen. Tragically, his mother repeatedly failed him in this way. Before a period of child counselling, Sascha presented as a sad, somewhat deadened little boy. After counselling, having been able to light up his therapist, he started to come alive and dared to love again.

Some parents may repeatedly 'misattune' to their child's feelings. (Misattunement means responding in a way that misses the point, or wrongly defines what the child is feeling.) Sometimes misattunement is a parent assuming that she knows what the child needs and feels, rather than listening and tuning in to him.

At other times misattunement happens through the parent's tone of voice or facial expression. Her tone, for example, may be one appropriate for feelings smaller than the ones the child is experiencing. If the child is feeling terrified, but her tone in response is one suitable for mild fear, that child is left alone with his terror. This is misattunement.

Just a little pain

You think mine 'just a little pain',
Some tiny itch or faintly ache,
Some little bottle on the shelf
With small cracked rim or smudgy side,
Some painted tear, or saddened song.

You think mine 'just a little pain',
Not worthy of a real concern
So offer 'just a little time',
A there-there pat or kindly 'Ah',
A token word through pretty smile.

Perhaps I used too little words?
Told you it all in jolly tones,
With happy mouth and skipping voice,
As if *I* spoke 'a little pain'?

I'll turn and tend my own wound now,
Because you saw 'a little pain'.

Margot Sunderland

Many parents are emotionally blind in one of the ways discussed above, because they have cut themselves off from too much of their own feeling life. This is because it is far too painful, or no one is helping *them* to process *their* troubling experiences.

When a parent repeatedly fails the child in these ways, the child learns that voicing his feelings with his parent makes him feel worse, not better. Or, looked at another way, by speaking his feelings, the child will evoke them more. The reasoning goes something like 'If I don't speak about this, I won't evoke the pain of it.' Consequently, the child establishes a fixed habit of private rather than shared experience of his feeling life. This is fuelled by a fear of a repeat of the past in the future. Because in the past his feelings have met with too many failed responses, he has come to believe that reaching out to someone with feeling is likely to lead to his feeling misunderstood, shamed, alienated, rejected, desperate or deeply alone all over again. What has happened with one key adult in the past all too easily gets generalised to all people. So, even if the child finds someone who can really listen, really understand, he may still withhold his feelings, owing to a firmly held belief that speaking them is a far too dangerous thing to do. As Masoliver (1999) says, 'If you no longer have hope that when you speak you will be understood, you cut off and start to live in a private world'.

Furthermore, if the adults in the child's life have not adequately helped him to digest and process his too difficult or too intense feelings, he learns to fear his emotions rather than to value them as clear signals for what he thinks, needs, wants, does not want and so on. Then, of course, the threatening, chaotic feeling force inside him can make his outer world a very difficult place to manage. It is extremely hard to make sense of your experiences properly when you have chaotic, confused or threatening feelings about them. In contrast, clear, sharply defined feeling helps you organise your experiences and so manage your being in the world.

At what age can bottling up feelings start?

In a psychological study called 'The Strange Situation Test' (Ainsworth *et al*, 1978) it was found that, by the age of one, some children are already dealing with their feelings by bottling them up.

During the test, when their mother left the room, some of the one-year-old children cried, in other words, they made a healthy protest. When their mother returned, they wanted a cuddle and also to stay very close to her, just for a minute or two. They let their mother know their distress, seemingly confident that she would hear and understand. In other words, they clearly felt it was of value to express their feelings with her. These children were named the 'Secure Attached Group'.

However, some of the one-year-olds in the study, did not cry. They seemed indifferent to their mother's comings and goings. They did not want to be picked up. Some even turned away from their mother when she returned. They showed no fear, distress or anger. They just got on with playing with their toys. The telling thing, however, was that, despite appearances, heart-rate measurements showed that they were actually feeling a very great deal – as much, in fact, as the secure children who cried. The difference was that they were simply not showing it. These children were then named the 'Avoidant Attached Group'. In short, they were already, at the age of one, self-holding.

Of course, developmentally and neurobiologically speaking, one-year-olds desperately need help with their distress. At this age, neuronal connections in their brains are still being formed for the capacity to regulate emotional arousal in later life. These particular neuronal connections can only be formed if the child has had a parent who can both amplify his positive feeling states, and calm and soothe them when they are distressed. Without a sound capacity for emotional regulation, a person can go through life psychobiochemically underaroused or overaroused. If a person is underaroused he can feel flat or dull and are prone to depression. If he is overaroused, he can be agitated, anxious or manic for much of the time, and unable to calm himself down. (For more on this, see Schore, 1994.)

When there is not enough space for a child's feelings because his mother is too busy with her own

Hayley, aged fourteen

Hayley was referred for counselling as she was extremely anxious and agitated most of the time. Hayley remembers an occasion when, as a little girl, out with her mother, she had badly hurt her knee. Hayley's first thought was 'Where is the nearest toilet, so I can get away from my mother and cry on my own?' She said her own sadness always seemed to trigger her mother's sadness, and so she would have to cope, not only with her own distress, but also with that of her mother. She felt frighteningly engulfed and swamped by her mother's grief.

Some parents fail to protect their child from the assault of their *own* neurosis. If a mother figure is too full of her own unworked-through feelings, she will be unable to be fully present for those of her child. Some parents are full of years of unprocessed grief or trauma. Others are regularly in a worried, anxious or agitated state, because *their own* parents were too full of unworked-through feelings and so they have never really known calm. Yet others are simply overburdened emotionally, overwhelmed from having to cope without the support of someone in their life to really soothe *them*. In short, if a parent is really going 'to be there' for her child's feelings, there needs to be someone in her life who 'is there' for hers.

A parent who is too full of her own feelings, can be very distressing for both a baby and a child. The infant can end up feeling her feelings as well as his own. This can lead to all manner of anxieties, nightmares, agitation, obsessions, inability to concentrate and other neurotic symptoms.

A child with a parent who is regularly anxious, depressed or angry all too often learns to 'self-hold', while in contrast his parent discharges, releases and offloads. This situation is exacerbated if the child has seen his parent expressing feeling in frightening ways: for example, he may have seen Daddy suddenly turn into a savage monster and scream at Mummy. In the face of the volatile or unpredictable parent, a child learns that it is not a good idea to express his own feelings, as this may set off more explosions in his parent. So he holds on to his own feelings and tries his best to be good. His volatile parent becomes the main performer on the family stage, while he takes the role of spectator.

Children of such parents sense that there is really no emotional space for them to express their feelings too. As one little girl who had an alcoholic father said, 'It's hard to have your feelings when someone else in the house is having theirs all the time.'

In short, his parent's feelings fill the house too much. They are in the air. Sometimes the child feels contaminated by them as if, defenceless, he has breathed them right in. It is no coincidence, therefore, that some children from such backgrounds are overweight. They often do the same with food as they do with other people's feelings. Their size is a physical manifestation of how emotionally burdened they are. Table 1 shows children's typical bottling-up responses to certain experiences of parental neuroses.

Nearest and dearest

You burst with shout, I swallow hard
No drain to flush away your hate
It's hanging in the air like a forgotten scarf
That no one quite dares throw away.
You shriek, and throw your rant
Against my silent backdrop,
(It highlighted you well);
Your face full fixed with soured time,
The slit of mouth, too long unkissed
Shrinking still,
A single line of tight from all the bitter years.

I, a faceless blank,
Held in unbreathing self,
Needed then, but now
Like a trained rat who knows no other way,
It's terribly hard to do anything else.

Margot Sunderland

Table 1 Children's common bottling-up responses to certain experiences of parental neuroses

Parental neurosis	Common responses and beliefs that can lead to the bottling up or actual repression of feelings in a child
An angry, irritable or hostile parent	'My feelings are dangerous. They may make Mummy lash out or criticise me, hate or reject me even more. So I'll concentrate on being good and just have "nice" feelings.'
An anxious parent	'I have to cope with all her anxieties. So I'll just put my feelings away, because it's too much to have to deal with my anxieties as well as hers.'
A depressed parent	'My strong feelings are dangerous, because my mother is so brittle. They might break or damage her in some way – the very person I need so much. So I'll just bottle them up and just have nice mild feelings.'
A parent who is often emotionally absent as she is preoccupied with her own emotional problems	'My painful feelings may send her even farther away or make her even cooler – so I'll just be very nice.' 'It is the absence of the mother that is now the danger.'(Freud, 1926)

Threats from any source arouse tendencies to withdraw from the source of threat and to approach the mother; what can such an infant do if the mother is . . . threatening? (De Zulueta, 1993, p82)

Children who bottle up their feelings in order to protect their parent

What living and buried speech is always vibrating here.
What howls restrained by decorum. (Walt Whitman)

Sometimes children decide to bottle up their feelings from a belief that 'My feelings are too strong and my Mummy is so fragile – so I'd better not have my feelings.' They fear their feelings may break or damage Mummy in some way. So, paradoxically, they end up holding themselves together to prevent their unstable parent from falling apart. Consequently, they may end up soothing the parent who is supposed to be soothing them.

Charlie, aged ten

Charlie got into protecting his Mummy from his too-big feelings. He did, however, tell her about some of the little ones. At a moment of amazing insight in counselling, having told a story about a too fragile bridge, he said, 'Something too big in me found something too little in my Mummy.'

Children who bottle up their feelings because their parents bottle up theirs

When parents cannot acknowledge their own feelings, it is hard for children to speak about theirs. From modelling themselves on their parents, some children learn that bottling up is what you do with feelings. Where there is an absence in a family of any expression of strong or passionate feeling, children may think that passionate emotion is somehow wrong or dangerous. In fact, such children from 'feeling taboo homes' often move into trying to experience life through thinking as opposed to feeling. Thinking becomes a regular and safe place of retreat from too strong feeling. Many such children become very clever because they live in their heads so much.

In other homes, some feelings are OK, such as joy or sadness, while others are taboo. The expression of fear and anger are common taboo feelings in many families. Thus the child gains no knowledge about the fact that saying you are scared or angry is often highly beneficial and important. Nor does he have a model of anger as healthy protest, when anger is expressed in a way that leads to a real connection with the other person, and a good and quick resolution.

Why helping a child with their troubled feelings is so important

Figure 5 (page 26) shows a car ferry. There is a traffic jam outside it, with all the cars waiting impatiently to get on board. As the cars wait, all the drivers get more and more tense, frustrated and angry with each other. This is similar to what happens to children who have a traffic jam of unworked-through feelings in their mind pressing to be processed. When feelings do not get worked through, there is an uneasy 'pile-up' of agitated emotional tension, making the child feel increasingly stressed, angry or anxious.

For children and adults alike, this emotional tension can be so disturbing that, often, it must be quickly explained away. A surge of too strong a feeling of missing someone, for example, can be labelled as 'I'm hungry. I need a Mars Bar'; a too strong impulse to cry can be labelled as 'I am really bored' or 'I'm fed up'. There is little solace to be had in such mislabelling, however, which ultimately does nothing to quell the surge of emotional pain and confusion that is not being addressed. Some children try to deal with their uneasy pile-up of feelings by distracting themselves via a computer game or television programme. Others do it by beating up someone in the playground, or equivalent antisocial behaviour. The intensity of the arousal cannot be managed in any other way. Psychobiochemically, the child is flooded. He is not bad or naughty, just plain overwhelmed.

Now look at Figure 6 (page 26), which depicts the car ferry of worked-through feelings. What it shows is similar to what happens in a child's mind when someone has helped him with the traffic of his too intense or troubled feelings: soothed him through them, providing quality time to try to really understand and to listen. If, consistently over time, a child has had this kind of help with his emotions, he will begin to view them as useful signals for action, and for what he wants and needs, rather than as a threat. He will know that feelings may be painful, but with help, when shared, they can be managed well. He will be able to 'stay with' a painful feeling and look it in the face, rather than needing to try to get rid of it quickly or to bind the too intense arousal into some neurotic symptom or destructive acting-out.

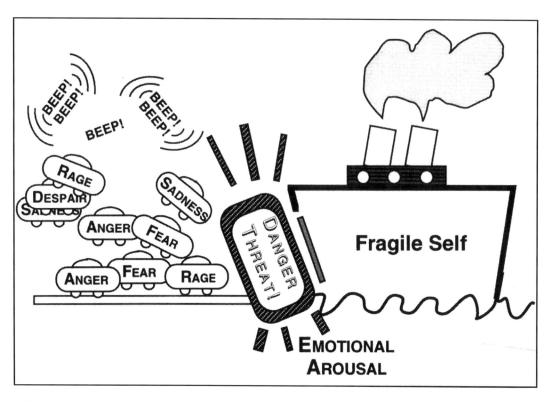

Figure 5 The car ferry of unworked-through feelings

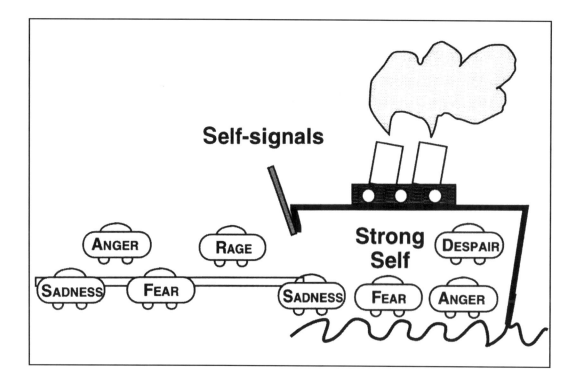

Figure 6 The car ferry of worked-through feelings

WHAT YOU CAN DO AFTER YOU HAVE READ *A NIFFLENOO CALLED NEVERMIND* TO THE CHILD

This section offers ideas for things to say and do after you have read this story to the child. The tasks, games and exercises are specifically designed to help a child to think about, express and further digest his feelings about the story's theme.

As previously discussed, children often cannot speak clearly and fully in everyday language about what they are feeling, but they can show or enact, draw or play out their feelings. Therefore, many of the exercises in this section offer support for creative, imaginative and playful ways of expression. They are also designed to inspire a child to respond further by telling his own stories.

In order that you avoid asking the child too many questions (children can soon feel interrogated), some exercises just require a tick in a box, or the choosing of a word or image from a selection.

Please note The tasks, games and exercises are not designed to be worked through in chronological order. Also, there are far too many to attempt them all in one go – the child would feel bombarded. So just pick the ones you think would be right for the child you are working with, taking into account his age, and how open he is to the subject matter. Instructions to the child are in tinted boxes.

✳ All about the 'too-full-of-feelings' feeling

Do you ever feel like any of these? (Tick if you do)

My head feels too full. ☐

My heart feels too full. ☐

There are too many feelings inside me to take in any more. ☐

I'd like to go to a place where I could scream and scream and scream. ☐

I'd just like to open the top of my head for a moment, so I can let out all my feelings. ☐

I sometimes wish I never had to feel anything ever again. ☐

I'm full of feelings, but I feel empty too. ☐

I can't stomach any more. ☐

I can't really be with what is happening around me, because there's too much feeling inside me. ☐

☀ Colourful feelings

On the picture of the boy or girl, draw the feelings you think you have been bottling up for a while. Use red for anger, green for fear, blue for sad, brown for a 'what's the point?' feeling and yellow for hurt.

Show how much of the feeling you have inside you. So, for example, if you are bottling up a lot of anger but not much sadness, draw a lot of red and a little bit of blue. Next, draw in the mouth.

Figure 7 Colourful feelings

29

✳ Five 'never mind' things

Draw or tell five things that have happened to you recently, to which you have said to yourself 'never mind', when really you *did* mind.

✳ Too-big feelings

Tick any of the following feelings that have got too big and strong inside you. (Because they have got so big and strong, it can mean that you are hurting too much inside). If it is more than one feeling, do more than one tick. If you have a too-big feeling that is not on the list, then write or draw that one.

Too much hate ☐
Too much anger ☐
Too much sadness ☐
Too much disappointment ☐
Too much love ☐
Too heart-broken ☐
Too much hurt ☐
Too much wanting something to happen which isn't happening ☐
Too much being all muddled up inside ☐
Too much fear ☐
Too much hating and loving someone all at the same time ☐
Too much worry ☐
Too much boredom ☐
Too much 'what's the point?' ☐
Too much jealousy ☐
Too much not liking myself ☐
Too much feeling miserable ☐
Too much shock ☐
Too much feeling I am bad ☐
Too much yucky feeling ☐
Too much messy feeling ☐
Too much horrid memory that I keep remembering ☐
Too much painful memory that I keep remembering ☐
Too much horrid, frightening thought ☐

✳ Water play with feelings

Through water play, talk to children about the feelings they are bottling up. This is usually irresistible, even for the most defended of children. Have some see-through jugs or bottles and fill up one with red water (using food colouring or paint), another with blue, another with green, another with yellow, and another with brown. Also have five empty bottles. Then say to the child: 'Red water is for angry feelings, blue water for sad feelings, green is for scared feelings, yellow is for hurt feelings, brown is for "What's the point?" feelings. Imagine these other bottles are you, and then pour into them how much of each of these feelings you have inside you at the moment.' (Alternatively, you can ask the child to put them all in one bottle, but watch how much of each is poured in.)

✳ Where you out your feelings

Children who bottle up their feelings often do have a concept of putting their feelings somewhere. A boy aged nine said to his counsellor, 'I keep my feelings in a tunnel. I just bring them out when I come and see you.' (This was a child diagnosed before the therapy as having autistic traits.) A child aged six said, 'My feelings for my mother are down at the bottom of the sea.'

When you keep all your feelings private and secret, and don't tell anyone what you are feeling, where does it feel like you are putting your feelings? Draw where you think you put them.

✳ **What might happen**

When a child is frightened to express his feelings, it may be a pointless task to try and 'prize them out of him'. It is often extremely annoying to the child, and may make him withdraw even further. Work instead to understand and empathise with his defences. Work with his fears of what might happen if he were really to tell you (or someone else) his feelings, as in this exercise.

What do you think might happen if you talk about or show the feelings you are bottling up inside? Tick if it is any of these:

I might explode ☐

I might smash something ☐

I'd never stop crying ☐

I might hit someone ☐

People might not like me any more ☐

I might damage/hurt/destroy the people I need/love ☐

My feelings might burn me up ☐

My feelings might drown me ☐

People might laugh at me ☐

People might think I am sissy and weak ☐

I'd lose my street cred ☐

Now draw the ones you have ticked. Draw what it would look like or feel like if it happened. Or, if your 'what might happen' is not on the list, draw your own.

✳ **Why saying that you are angry feels so frightening**

What do you think might happen if you let go of the anger you are bottling up inside, and told people what you really felt? Tick if it is any of these:

People will hear ☐

Everyone will look at me ☐

I will scare people ☐

I'll drive everyone away ☐

I'll be hated ☐

They'll see something very nasty in me, and I'll see it, too ☐

People will be disgusted ☐

I will turn into some awful monster ☐

I'll go out of control ☐

The anger will never stop ☐

I might really hurt someone ☐

The other person might die ☐

I might die ☐

They'll say I'm mad ☐

✳ Why anger is frightening

What do you think has made anger so frightening for you?
◎ Draw anger

◎ Now draw somebody being angry

◎ Now draw or show in sandplay a time when somebody's anger was frightening

◎ Finish these sentences:

I think anger is _____

If somebody gets very angry then what will happen is _____

If I get very angry then what will happen is _____

☀ Feelings that are spoiling your life

Colour in any of the feelings that you are feeling in your life at the moment, and that are preventing you from having a nice time.

Figure 8 Feelings that are spoiling your life

✳ **What might happen**
Draw a picture to end all of these sentences

If I let out my sadness, what might happen is . . .	If I let out my anger, what might happen is . . .
If I let out my fear, what might happen is . . .	If I cry, what might happen is . . .

✳ **My too-full dreams**

In bad dreams about something being too full, there is often a feeling that there is no escape from this fullness, and so it is frightening. Dreams like this are often telling the dreamer that he feels too full of feelings, or that he is too full of someone else's feelings as well as his own.

◎ Have you ever had a bad dream about something being too full?
◎ How did the dream go?
Draw it if you like.

✳ Make a picture of feelings

Think of feelings, thoughts or memories that you don't seem to be able to get out of your mind.
Mould them using Play-Doh, or draw them. Use speech or thought bubbles if it helps.

✳ Traffic jams of feelings

One way to explain to children about what can go wrong if they bottle up feelings is to tell them about the car ferry and its traffic jams. So, in explaining to a child how trying to deal with all their feelings all by themselves doesn't work that well, show the child the car ferry pictures in Figures 5 and 6. Then you could say something like this:

Think of a car ferry, like the one in this picture. It has a traffic jam of cars outside, all waiting to get in and park. But, as they wait, all the drivers get more and more cross with each other. Well, this is a bit like what happens if you have a traffic jam of bottled-up feelings inside you. When feelings don't get properly felt and thought about, there can be a build-up of horrid tension and confusion inside. This is because clear, sorted-out feeling is the main way we understand and manage what goes on in our lives. But to get rid of the traffic jam of feelings inside you, you need someone's help. Otherwise, you may end up going round and round in circles, and get more and more muddled inside, with more tension and more pain.

☀ Too many feelings

When you have too many feelings inside, does your mind ever feel like one or more of these? If so, colour them in. If you can't find something close to what you feel, draw your own feeling in the empty box.

Figure 9
Too many feelings

✳ Little feelings and big feelings

People can have little feelings, medium-sized feelings, or big feelings. Sometimes feelings get just too big and too strong and then they can feel very painful and frightening. When your feelings get too strong, does it ever feel that your mind or your body is like one or more of the pictures? If so, colour them in.

A storm	A raging sea	A flood
A frightening thick fog	A hideous monster	A fire
A volcano	An earthquake	An avalanche

Figure 10
Little feelings
and big feelings

✳ Put down all that baggage at last

Talk to the child about how, when you find someone you can really trust and you tell them the feelings you have been bottling up inside, it can feel great. It can be like laying down the heaviest suitcase you've been carrying, all by yourself, for far too long. It can be like feeling very warm inside. It can be like saying, 'You do the worrying now. I'm too tired to do it on my own any more.'

You might use the story of Pandora's Box to help you:

> The jar was almost empty; everything that was cruel, violent or swift had left it. All that was left, right at the bottom, was a little thing [which] was calm and assured. It was hope. (Comte, 1994, p158)

> I broke down and cried – I who had been unable to cry for so long, who for so many months had sought in vain the comfort of tears. Now at last they flowed freely, dissolving the tension in my back, my chest, and my shoulders. I cried for a long time. I revelled in the storm. (Cardinal, 1993, p32)

✳ The power of saying no

This game is designed for children who say 'Yes' when they actually want to say 'No'. What happens is that you say 'Yes' quietly, and they then say, 'No' to your 'Yes', louder than your 'Yes'. And then you say, 'Yes' louder than their 'No'. And then they say 'No', louder than your 'Yes', and so on, until they are really loud and forceful. It is fun, but they will also taste what it is like to feel assertive.

Then do a role-play where you enact a bullying child and they practise standing up to you and saying 'No'. For example:

> *Bully:* 'Give me your sweets!'
> *Child:* 'No, I don't want to!'
> *Bully:* 'Get off the swing, I want it.'
> *Child:* 'No, I won't.'

You can then give feedback to the child about how he did and how he can come across as more convincingly assertive – in his body language, tone and choice of words.

✳ Bottling up warm feelings is a waste

This exercise involves things to say to children about the waste of bottling up warm or lovely feelings. You can play this out with little characters in sandplay to help engage the child:

You can bottle up warm feelings as well as painful feelings. Bottling up warm feelings means not telling someone about something you love about the world, or about something good in your life, or about something funny. It can mean not telling someone you like them, or love them, or that you really enjoy being their friend. It can mean not giving someone a hug when you feel like it. This is a waste. If you don't share these things, you are worse off, and so is the other person. If you do share them, the other person feels warm and it will probably make you feel warm too. Lovely feelings are often known as warm, fuzzy feelings. So saying to someone, 'I really like playing with you' is giving someone a 'warm fuzzy'. ['Warm fuzzies' were first named by Claude Steiner in his story *The Original Warm Fuzzy Tale*.] A smile is also giving someone a warm fuzzy. Warm fuzzy feelings don't take too well to being bottled up. They often die off that way.

✳ Your memories

What lovely memories have you got inside your mind?
Draw one or two of your favourites.

✳ To bottle up or not to bottle up

This exercise is for children who both want, and fear asking for, help with their too difficult feelings. Some children who are self-holding want to find someone who is big enough and strong enough and understanding enough to help them with their feelings. But they are wary, too, and think that maybe it is best just to carry on self-holding. Such children can feel very understood, if they have this ambivalence acknowledged. You could say something such as:

> Unexpressed feelings are like tangled knitting wool. They can get all mixed up inside you. One part of you may want to sort out the tangle, to feel your feelings, to tell someone about them, while another part of you may be very frightened of doing this, and so you carry on holding on to the tangled knitting all by yourself.

You could play this out with characters in sandplay to help engage the child. Use actual tangled knitting wool.

You may then ask them, 'How big is the part of you that wants to get some help with the too difficult feelings inside you? How big is the part of you which wants to keep them all to yourself?' 'Show me on paper'.

✳ The good and the bad things about telling someone what you feel

What would be good about telling someone about your feelings? Write or draw it here.	
What would be good about keeping on bottling them up and dealing with them all by yourself? Write or draw it here.	
What would be bad about telling someone about your feelings? Write or draw it here.	
What would be bad about keeping on bottling them up and dealing with them all by yourself? Write or draw it here.	

The neurotic conflict, by definition, is one between a tendency striving for discharge and another tendency that tries to prevent this discharge. (Fenichel, 1990, p129)

CONSIDERING FURTHER COUNSELLING OR THERAPY FOR CHILDREN WHO BOTTLE UP THEIR FEELINGS

What can happen in later life to children who continue to bottle up their feelings

Because they do not share what they feel, for these children relationships may tend to be far less fulfilling, in terms of experiencing a real intimacy. Presenting as a solely thinking self, rather than a thinking-feeling self, usually makes a person difficult to be with for any length of time. People pick up that something is missing here, a vital dimension of humanness, a fully felt life. People who never share their more private feelings in a close relationship can also be seen as withholding, frustrating or boring.

Some people who have bottled-up feelings all their life may at some point break out 'with dark and violent force . . . a black angry inner flood,' as Padel (1995, p50) calls it. This 'angry flood' may be turned against oneself or other people. Others develop a serious stress-related illness. High levels of cortisol (a stress hormone) tend to be released in people who choose to keep their painful feelings a private affair. High levels of cortisol are extremely detrimental to the immune system.

For some people, the repression of painful feelings can work well for years, and then at some point, the repression breaks down. Some breakdowns in adulthood are breakdowns of repression, after years and years of bottling up feelings. 'Our most intense feelings are involuntary reactions; we cannot decide when they will erupt' (Goleman, 1996, p293).

Why counselling or therapy for children who bottle up their feelings ?

Good counselling or therapy gives the child an intense experience of a soothing empathic other. Most children find this such a nourishing experience, that later on in life, in times of emotional pain, they will want to seek out someone to talk to about their painful feelings, rather than bottling them up so that they leak out in any manner of neurotic symptoms. They will want friends and intimates who are naturally empathic, rather than choosing people who attack, dismiss or avoid their talking about feelings. With such 'emotional self-care', both people and events are far less likely to be experienced as overwhelming, frightening or dangerous.

Of course, many children who have bottled up their feelings for a long time, are not going to want to suddenly start talking about them. With such children there is often a deep mistrust. However, a long-term relationship with a therapist or counsellor can provide many children with the necessary safety and conditions in which they will dare to let go. Child therapists and counsellors have undergone their own intensive therapy in order to know and work through their own deep levels of pain. Children very quickly sense this: that the therapist is not frightened by very intense or very painful feelings. It makes them feel safe, whereas, metaphorically speaking, if there is no sense of a lifeboat, such wary children will not just jump into the stormy sea.

For children who are bottling up a great deal of grief, fear or anger, the regular one or more hourly sessions each week can be an immense support for 'unbottling'. If you are seven years old, say, and have never really fully digested any of your painful feelings, you have a lot of digesting to do. A 'one-off' or occasional session will not provide the child with the psychological holding he needs to really feel safe enough to go into his painful feelings.

For some children like Nevermind, the sheer pressure from having held in their feelings for so long can mean that, when they do eventually let go, there may be some very noisy, lengthy explosions of feeling. The therapist is trained to be able to stay with these, offering empathy, containment and psychological holding. Someone who is untrained may be frightened at the sheer intensity of feelings, and try to deflect them or stop them in some way.

Emma, aged six

At school, Emma had learning difficulties. She would bottle up her feelings for most of the day. Then, suddenly, she would half-scream, for no apparent reason, then go back to being a 'too good' child. After two years of doing this, she was offered therapy. In therapy she would let herself really scream and really shake with fear. She did it facing the therapist, who held both her hands. Emma had been too frightened by the intensity of her own fear to do it on her own, yet it had been leaking out every so often and making it impossible for her to concentrate on her schoolwork. The therapist discovered that, at one time, Emma had been sent to a children's home. As punishment on several occasions, she had been locked in a cupboard. She had been too frightened to cry out.

As we have seen, children can persistently bottle up feelings because expressing feelings was at one time linked to something awful, such as being shamed, criticised or ignored. When they do let go in therapy, and scream or shout, wail or express feelings of terrible hurt or disappointment, it can come as a real surprise and great relief that they feel good, and nothing and no one has got damaged or destroyed in the process.

We end by quoting some of the things that children who used to bottle up their feelings have said about counselling or therapy:

Ann, aged eleven

'There were all my sad feelings and then there was the telling about all my sad feelings, and the one helped the other very much.'

Bee, aged twelve

Bee used to bottle up her feelings. Now she cannot wait for her counselling session each week:
'I need you to know what I am feeling, to keep knowing it, and knowing it and knowing it. If you don't, I'm all alone with feeling bad. And the all-alone is worse than the feeling bad.'

Simon, aged twelve

When he was ten, Simon's mother took in a lover who beat up Simon. The social services said she must ask her lover to move out, as Simon was at risk. She refused. So Simon, for his own safety, was put into care. Simon felt intensely hurt. It felt like his mother had chosen her lover over him. He fell into a terrible depression. He spoke to no one about his feelings. After two years of awful bottling up and refusing to speak, he agreed to see a therapist.
One day, after months of therapy, he dared to let out his anger. Initially, he was terrified. He said that, every time he got angry, he just filled up again with more anger. He thought this process would go on for ever. Then one day he realised that he was empty of all his anger. One day he said, 'It's funny you know, for the first time today, I heard the birds singing, and smelt the flowers and saw the beauty of the hills behind the house.' Before this, his bottled up anger and hurt had simply blocked the view to this, to all the beauty and goodness in his world.

BIBLIOGRAPHY

Ainsworth MDS, Blehar MC, Waters E & Wall S, 1978, *Patterns of Attachment: A Psychological Study of The Strange Situation*, Lawrence Erlbaum Associates, Hillsdale, NJ.

Bar-Levav R, 1988, *Thinking in the Shadow of Feelings*, Simon & Schuster, New York.

Blume ES, 1990, *Secret Survivors: Uncovering Incest and its After Effects in Women*, John Wiley, Chichester/New York.

Bowlby J, 1988, *A Secure Base: Clinical Applications of Attachment Theory*, Routledge, London.

Cardinal M, 1993, *The Words to Say It: An Autobiographical Novel* (Goodheart P, trans), Women's Press, London (originally published in French, 1975).

Comte F, 1994, *The Wordsworth Dictionary of Mythology* (Goring A, trans), Wordsworth Editions, Ware (originally published in French, 1988).

De Zulueta F, 1993, *From Pain to Violence: The Traumatic Roots of Destructiveness*, Whurr, London.

Dostoevsky F M, 1991, *Notes from the Underground* (Kentish J, trans), Oxford University Press, Oxford.

Euripedes, 1994, *Plays: One* (Medea; The Phoenician Women; The Bacchae), Methuen, London.

Fenichel O, 1990, *The Psychoanalytic Theory of Neurosis*, Routledge, London.

Freud S, 1915, 'Repression', pp139-57 in *On Metapsychology: The Theory of Psychoanalysis*, Vol 11 of *The Penguin Freud Library* (Richards A & Strachey J, eds, Strachey J, trans), 1991, Penguin, Harmondsworth.

Freud S, 1926, 'Inhibitions, Symptoms and Anxiety', pp237-333 in *On Psychopathology, Inhibitions, Symptoms and Anxiety*, Vol 10 of *The Penguin Freud Library* (Richards A & Strachey J, eds, Strachey J, trans), 1979, Penguin, Harmondsworth.

Galloway J, 1996, 'The Trick Is to Keep Breathing', pp132-40 in Dunn S, Morrison B & Roberts M (eds), *Mind Readings – Writers' Journeys Through Mental States*, Minerva, London.

Goleman D, 1996, *Emotional Intelligence*, Bloomsbury, London.

Herman N, 1987, *Why Psychotherapy?* Free Association Books, London.

Janov A, 1987, *The Feeling Child: Affective Development Reconsidered*, Haworth Press, New York.

Kaplan L, 1978, *Oneness and Separateness: From Infant to Individual*, Touchstone, New York.

Kohut H & Wolf ES, 1978, 'The Disorders of the Self and Their Treatment', *International Journal of Psycho-Analysis*, 59: pp413-24.

Lowen A, 1975, *Bioenergetics*, Penguin, Harmondsworth.

McDougall J, 1989, *Theatres of the Body: A Psychoanalytical Approach to Psychosomatic Illness*, Free Association Books, London.

Martin P, 1997, *The Sickening Mind*, Harper Collins, London.

Masoliver C, 1999, 'Delusions: Metaphor or Madness', lecture given at The Arbours Association, 6 Church Lane, London N8.

Nakhla F & Jackson G, 1993, *Picking Up the Pieces*, Yale University Press, New Haven.

Neruda P, 1975, *Selected Poems*, Penguin, Harmondsworth.

Okri B, 1991, *The Famished Road*, Cape, London.

Padel R, 1995, *Whom Gods Destroy: Elements of Greek and Tragic Madness*, Princeton University Press, Princeton, NJ.

Resnick R, 1993, Personal communication during couples therapy training at the Metanoia Trust, London.

Ritsos Y, 1974, *Collected Poems*, (Stangos N, trans), Penguin, Harmondsworth.

Schore A, 1994, *Affection Regulation and the Origin of Self: The Neurobiology of Emotional Development*, Lawrence Erlbaum Associates, Hillsdale, NJ.

Segal J, 1985, *Phantasy in Everyday Life: A Psychoanalytical Approach to Understanding Ourselves*, Penguin, Harmondsworth.

Steiner C, 1984, *The Original Warm Fuzzy Tale*, Jalmar Press.

Sunderland M, 1993, *Draw On Your Emotions*, Speechmark Publishing/ Winslow Press, Bicester.

Sunderland M, 2000, *Using Story Telling as a Therapeutic Tool with Children*, Speechmark Publishing/Winslow Press, Bicester.

Whitman W, 1995, *Leaves of Grass*, Penguin Classics, Harmondsworth.

Williamson M, 1992, *A Return To Love*, Random House, New York.

Winnicott DW, 1965, 'The Psychology of Madness: A Contribution from Psycho-Analysis', in Winnicott C, Shepherd R & Davis M (eds), *DW Winnicott: Psycho-Analytic Explorations*, 1989, Karnac, London.

Winnicott DW, 1988, *Human Nature*, Free Association Books, London.